PICTURES
FROM A MEDIAEVAL
BIBLE

Copyright © 1959 by James Strachan. All rights reserved
Library of Congress catalog card number: 61 — 10568
First published in Great Britain in 1959 by Darwen Finlayson Ltd.
First published in the United States in 1961 by the Beacon Press
Printed in the United States of America

Second printing, October 1961

PICTURES
FROM A MEDIAEVAL
BIBLE

Commentary by
JAMES STRACHAN

BEACON PRESS

BOSTON

CONTENTS

TABLE OF BIBLICAL CONTENTS

OLD TESTAMENT

APOCRYPHA

NEW TESTAMENT

Preface

THE reception accorded to my book on *Early Bible Illustrations* (Cambridge University Press, 1957) leads me to think that it brought to light a certain amount of buried treasure that otherwise would have remained hidden away in library shelves. The object of the present book is to display the treasure to better advantage. I am indebted to the University Press for their encouragement to proceed with this more popular work.

Drawn to illustrate the text of one of the earliest printed bibles, the pictures of the Cologne Bible retain their primitive simplicity and effectiveness. I have endeavoured to keep the descriptive notes within bounds, referring each picture however to chapter and verse in the hope that readers may study the relevant passages in the Bible for themselves.

The illustrations are taken from one or other of the copies of the Cologne Bible in the Library of the British and Foreign Bible Society, to whom my thanks are due for these facilities. The photography was done by R. B. Fleming & Co. Ltd., and the blocks were made by The Gade Engraving Co. Ltd., of Watford.

JAMES STRACHAN

Farnham Common, April 1959.

INTRODUCTION: THE COLOGNE BIBLE ILLUSTRATIONS

PRINTING with movable type was the invention of John Gutenberg of Mainz about 500 years ago. One of the first books he printed was the Bible in Latin, the version known as the Vulgate, which had been commonly used in the Roman Catholic Church for something like a thousand years. It had been translated out of Greek and Hebrew by Jerome, a learned and devoted scholar who lived around 400 A.D., in the latter days of the Western Roman Empire.

Gutenberg, like many another inventor, died a poor man; but the knowledge of his invention spread rapidly, first throughout Germany and then to Italy and France. Those were the days when a new interest in the works of the ancient Greek and Roman writers was showing itself in Western Europe, and printing presses were set up in many cities to meet the new demand. At that time, most people who could read at all read Latin, a language which had been spoken over most of Europe in the time of Jerome. It had never been fully established in Northern Europe and there in the course of a thousand years it was supplanted by German and other Teutonic tongues. In Southern Europe it had itself developed into languages derived from Latin, such as Italian, Spanish and French. Latin, however, remained the language of the Church, and the clergy were able to make good use of the newly printed Latin bibles.

In 1466 a printed German bible was put on sale at Strassburg, followed by another a few years later. These bibles in the common tongue were meant, we may suppose, for the common people; but the trouble was that few of the common people could read. Now it so happened that, a whole generation before Gutenberg, the art of printing drawings in black and white had reached Europe from China, where it had long been practised. The process consisted of cutting into the surface of a block of wood, so as to show up the lines of the drawing in relief, then inking the block and using it as a stamp, in much the same way as lino-blocks are commonly used in schools today. Before ordinary printing, woodcuts, as these block prints were called, were used to make whole books of pictures of this kind, and some on biblical subjects were helpful to the clergy in the instruction of their flocks.

When new bibles in the common tongue were printed, a few illustrations to go with the text were particularly welcome. When the old monks used to copy out the scriptures by hand, they often enriched their written work by drawing or painting an elaborate initial letter to begin a new book or a new chapter. Sometimes in the case of letters like O or P they could fill the open space with a little picture suggested by the story they might be telling. Gunther Zainer's German bible printed at Augsburg about 1475 had 71 woodcuts of these initial letters, most of the books of the Bible being headed in this way. The idea soon spread and in the two Bibles printed at Cologne between 1478 and 1480 the illustrations are a very special feature. They are no longer just initial letters, but are introduced at the right places in the text to tell their story most effectively. The pages are printed in parallel columns and with only two exceptions the illustrations extend over both columns, measuring $7\frac{1}{4}$ inches in width and $4\frac{3}{4}$ inches in depth.

The preface of the Cologne bible tells us that in order to make the text easier to understand and to give encouragement to the reader, here and there pictures are introduced, "just as paintings have for a long time been a feature of churches and monasteries". So far as we know they are not copied from wall paintings in these old buildings. There is a manuscript bible in the Berlin State Library with pictures very like those of the Cologne Bibles, possibly by the same artist. His name seems to have been Cleve or Van Cleef. Nothing is known about him for certain, but an artist family of that name flourished in Antwerp a hundred years later.

From the style of his landscapes it seems almost certain that he had lived in Holland or Belgium.

There were two Cologne bibles between 1478 and 1480, one following close after the other. The later one was in the Low Saxon dialect and the earlier in the dialect of the Lower Rhine, very like Dutch. The same wood-blocks were used, except that for the second printing some errors in the first were corrected, and in the second ten more illustrations were added, making 123 all told.

The Cologne bibles are of particular importance because their illustrations served as patterns for whole series of illustrations in later bibles in German, Italian, Czech (or Bohemian), French, Dutch and English, including the Great Bible of Henry VIII which came out in 1539. Before 1500, similar illustrations had been brought into Latin bibles as well. Nowadays most countries have laws to forbid the copying of letterpress or illustrations by one printer from another, except with permission, for which payment is usually made. In the early days of printing there was no such protection for authors, artists, or their publishers. Ilustrations could very readily be transferred from one book to another and a favourite set of drawings, such as appeared first in the Cologne bibles, was copied by other printers again and again. Sometimes the copying was far from intelligent and the illustrations that suffered in this way became more corrupt and less valuable as time went on; unless, as sometimes happened, the series was taken in hand by a real artist and restored to health and strength.

THE OLD TESTAMENT

THE CREATION FINISHED.   *Genesis i and ii.*
This is the large headpiece for Genesis. In the centre Eve
is being taken from Adam's side as he lies in a deep sleep.
The animal and plant creations abound in the country
around and there are living creatures in the encircling sea.
The sun, moon and stars can be seen in the "firmament".
The Lord on high, surrounded by a heavenly choir, breathes
into the man the breath of life, "so that man became a
living soul".

Ccie begint Genesis dat ierste weck: en
is vā der schepins der werlt: en des mysche-
N dem anbegyn schoep got he
mell en erde. Met die erde was
ledich en ydell. en die dupster
nisse waren vp dē aensicht des
affgronts ★ dat is vp den aen
sicht der elementen die do wa
ren vniuerscheiden. J en die geist gaets wart
genoirt bauen die waeter. En got die sprak.
Dat licht werder: en licht wart. En got
die sach dat dat licht guet was: en hij teil-
den dat lichte van der dupsternissen: en dat
licht noemde hi den dach: en die dustternisse
die nacht en die auent en morgen wart eyn
dach. En got die sprak. Dat firmament

werde in den middel der water. en by schep
den die waeter van den waeteren. En got
maekte dat firmamēt en teildā die water
die. dar warē vnder dē firmamēt. van dē die
dar warē bauē dē firmamēt en dat geschach
also En got noemde dat firmamēt dē hemel
en dat wart die auent en die morgen die an
der dach. En got sprak ander werff. De water
die vnder dē hemel sin werden vergadert an
ein stat: en verschyne die doricheit. En dat
geschach also. ende got hete die doricheyt
dat ertrik en die vergadeange der water he
te hi dat mer: en got sach dat dat gud was
en sprak. Die erde grote groiende krupt en
dat saet mask: ende holt dat appel dreghe
na sinen kunne: des saet sy in em seliff vp dri

1

ADAM AND EVE.   *Genesis iii.*
   As not infrequently happens, two scenes from the story
are shown in the same frame. First we have Adam and Eve
in the Garden, and the serpent, with a human face, tempting
Eve to eat the forbidden fruit. The Lord God speaks from
above and Adam appears to listen. Then on the other side
we seen Adam and Eve turned out of the Garden by the
angel with the flaming sword. The contrast between the
fertility of the Garden and the barrenness of the outside
wilderness is well brought out.

CAIN AND ABEL.   *Genesis iv* 1-15.
   This is from the second edition.
   In the first edition Cain was labelled CAIEM. The unneces-
sary letter E was chiselled off the wood block before it was
used for the next edition. Three episodes are shown here.
On the left are Cain and Abel sacrificing, Abel's sacrifice
being highly successful while Cain's turns out a flop. In the
centre Cain murders Abel, using the jawbone of a large
animal as a club. On the right the Lord speaks to Cain as he
prepares to leave the country.

2

3

NOAH'S ARK.   *Genesis vi to viii.*
This must be near the end of the Flood, for while Noah
is looking out at one side to receive the dove with the olive
leaf, the church spires and mountain tops are appearing at
the other. The human family can be seen through the open
door, while the smaller animals are stretching their legs on
the deck and the birds are interested in the cat on the roof.
The merman and the mermaid are a curious fancy.

THE BUILDING OF BABEL.   *Genesis xi 1-9.*
The chiselling of the stone and the handling of the bricks
and mortar seem to be according to the practices of 1478.

4

5

MELCHIZEDEK MEETING ABRAHAM. *Genesis xiv* 17-24.
Abraham, partially clad in armour, is returning with his allies from a successful pursuit of the raiders from Mesopotamia who had carried off his nephew Lot. He is met at the gate of Salem (or Jerusalem) by the King, Melchizedek, who was also a priest, and who presents Abraham with bread and wine. It is perhaps a little unfortunate that the tree in the background has been placed in line with the cup. The inscription on the banner seems to correspond with "Eshcol", the name of one of Abraham's allies.

ABRAHAM'S VISITORS. *Genesis xviii* 1-8.
Abraham, sitting in his tent door in the heat of the day, saw three men approaching and ran to welcome them, and, as it turned out, he "entertained angels unawares". The tree, which comes into the story, is shown, but the "tent-door" looks like the porch of a modern mansion. The rabbit peeping out suggests that the meeting is some distance from the town.

6

7

ABRAHAM AND ISAAC.   *Genesis xxii* 1-14.

In the foreground we have Isaac carrying the wood and Abraham with the pot of fire to set it alight, and his sword. Behind, an angel holds back the sword from striking, and the ram is waiting, not yet caught in the thicket. The walled city in the background and the windmill are somewhat unexpected.

ISAAC AND JACOB.   *Genesis xxvii.*

Isaac is old and blind and has asked Esau, his elder son, to hunt for venison, bring him "savoury meat", and receive his blessing. Jacob, the younger son, put up to it by Rebekah, comes with a dish of goat's flesh, wearing goatskin gloves so as to appear hairy like his brother. He receives the blessing instead.

All four characters are shown. Esau in the distance with bow and arrow is blowing a horn, perhaps to rouse the deer in the wood. Anyhow the rabbit in the foreground is taking no chances.

8

9

JACOB'S DREAM.   *Genesis xxviii* 10-22.
The dream of the ladder reaching from earth to heaven, with angels going to and fro and the Lord speaking from above, took place at Luz or Bethel, which is on the Palestine plateau. The artist has placed it by the sea or on a lake or large river like the Rhine, with castellated buildings, and Jacob's costume is in keeping with these surroundings.

JOSEPH AND THE PIT.   *Genesis xxxvii* 18-28.
The chapter tells the story of how Joseph's dreams offended his brethren and how they took their revenge, first by casting him into a pit and then taking him from it to sell him into slavery in Egypt. The pit, we are told, was a dry well.

The eleven brothers are in the picture, with some of their sheep and the sheep-dog which has a spiky collar to protect him in any encounter with a wolf. The Ishmaelites on their way to Egypt are seen approaching with a guard on horseback and at least one camel.

The signature of the artist CLEVE is to be seen on a garment towards the left. This is the only picture on which it occurs.

10

11

JOSEPH CAST INTO PRISON. *Genesis* xxxix 1-20.
Potiphar, who after all was only "captain of the guard", has been given a crown and a sceptre. His wife seems to be looking on with satisfaction, holding the incriminating garment slung over her arm.

PHARAOH'S DREAM. *Genesis* xli 1-4.
We have a glimpse of Pharaoh's bedroom. On the left we see the seven fat kine which came up out of the river and are now feeding in a meadow; on the right the seven lean kine still by the river's brink. How the seven lean kine devoured the seven fat kine, and what this was taken to mean and how it all worked out in the fortunes of Joseph and Pharaoh are told in the rest of this long and entertaining chapter.

12

13

JOSEPH'S BROTHERS SEEKING TO BUY CORN.   *Gen. xlii* 1-20.
The ten brothers have come into Egypt leaving Benjamin
at home with their father Jacob. Joseph speaks to them
roughly, but treats them generously on the whole and
demands that on their return they produce Benjamin.

THE CUP IN BENJAMIN'S SACK.   *Genesis xlii* 43-*xliv* 13.
There are two scenes here; on the left the brothers being
entertained and on the right the finding of the cup which
Joseph had smuggled into Benjamin's sack. The dog seems
interested in other things.

14

15

DEPARTURE OF THE BRETHREN AGAIN.   *Genesis xlv* 14-24.
By this time Joseph had made himself known to his brethren and told Pharaoh about them. With Pharaoh's approval they are setting out for Canaan once more, to bring their father to Egypt while the famine lasts. The asses are well laden and Joseph is taking a tearful farewell of Benjamin. His last words to the others were "See that ye fall not out by the way".

JACOB'S ARRIVAL IN EGYPT.   *Genesis xlvii* 1-10.
Joseph is kneeling before Pharaoh to present some of his brothers, while Jacob is waiting his turn in the carriage and pair, followed by his large family.

16

17

JACOB'S BLESSING.   *Genesis xlix.*

All twelve sons are gathered to hear their father's prophecies regarding each of them and to receive his blessing.

BURIAL OF JACOB.   *Genesis l 1-13.*

Jacob expressed a wish to be buried in the cave of Machpelah in the land of Canaan with Abraham and Sarah, Isaac and Rebekah and his own first wife, Leah. Joseph and his other sons, with help from the Egyptians, carried out his request.

18

19

ISRAEL IN EGYPT.   *Genesis l 26 to Exodus i 22.*

A version of this picture appears at the head of Exodus in a great many old Bibles. On the left Joseph is being placed in a coffin, as stated in the last verse of Genesis. On the right the Pharaoh "which knew not Joseph" is instructing the midwives Shiphra and Puah to stifle the male children at birth. They evaded the order, and in the background the Egyptians are seen drowning the children in the Nile.

THE INFANT MOSES.   *Exodus ii 1-10.*

Again three scenes in one picture. In the background Moses' parents are launching the "ark of bulrushes" on the Nile. On the left it is being found by Pharaoh and his daughter. On the right Moses, perhaps a little older, is getting on famously with Pharaoh.

20

21

THE BURNING BUSH.   *Exodus iii 1-iv 9.*
Moses and his dog, while tending his herds and flocks,
have their attention drawn to the burning bush, from which
God speaks. Moses has dropped his rod and is pulling off a
shoe. In the background we see the experiment with the rod
described in Chapter iv, the dog being still interested.

All the old pictures of Moses represent him as having
small horns. The Hebrew word for horns is very like that
for rays of light and when the Bible tells us (in Exodus
xxxiv, 29) that Moses came down from Mt. Sinai with a
beaming face, Jerome thought it meant that he had horns,
and translated it accordingly. Though the incident took place
about half way through the career of Moses, the artists
found the horns a useful distinguishing mark and for a
thousand years they persisted in giving Moses horns wher-
ever he appears, from early manhood onwards.

THE FIRST PLAGUE.   *Exodus vii 8-25.*
There are two episodes here. On the left Aaron is giving a
demonstration of magic power by casting down his rod and
turning it into a serpent. Then when the Egyptian magicians
turn their rods into serpents also, Aaron's serpent swallows
them up. This procedure proving ineffective, Moses is seen
on the right bringing on the first plague, smiting the river
with the rod and turning the water into blood, so that the
fish died and the river stank and there was blood throughout
the land of Egypt.

22

23

THE SECOND PLAGUE.   *Exodus viii* 1-13.
On the left, Moses is receiving instructions from the Lord and passing them on to Aaron. On the right, frogs everywhere!

THE PLAGUE OF FLIES.   *Exodus viii* 20-24.
This plague was designed to torment the Egyptians, but the farm animals seem to be getting the worst of it. The infliction of a murrain on the cattle comes in the next chapter, Exodus ix 1-7.

24

25

THE PLAGUE OF BOILS AND BLAINS.   *Exodus ix* 8-12.
Moses is directed to take handfuls of ashes of the furnace
and sprinkle them towards heaven, thereby producing boils
and blains upon man and beast.

THE PLAGUE OF HAIL.   *Exodus ix* 13-35.
The terrific hailstorm accompanied by thunder and fire
"which ran along upon the ground".

26

27

THE PLAGUE OF LOCUSTS.   *Exodus* X 12-15.
    The locusts brought by a strong east wind are devouring
the vegetation, and Pharaoh is powerless.

THE FINAL PLAGUES: *Exodus* X 21-23 *and* xi 1-10.
DARKNESS AND SLAUGHTER OF THE FIRSTBORN.
    The darkness "which may be felt" comes in the right half
of the picture. On the left are scenes of misery and lamentation. In the Bible there is confusion between two accounts
of the same story and the artist has found the story difficult
to portray.

28

29

THE PASSOVER.   *Exodus xii* 11-14.

The Israelites, on the point of departure from Egypt, observe the first Feast of the Passover as directed: "with your loins girded, your shoes on your feet, and your staff in your hand; and ye shall eat it in haste".

THE CROSSING OF THE RED SEA.   *Exodus xiv* 21-31.

The Israelites led by Moses have arrived on the far side with their cattle and at least one camel. The vast Egyptian army behind is overwhelmed.

30

31

THE SONG OF MIRIAM AND   *Exodus xv* 20-26.
THE WATERS OF MARAH.

On the left Miriam, "the sister of Aaron" (Aaron seems to be in the picture also), is followed by a procession of women celebrating their deliverance on the timbrel and other musical instruments. "Sing ye to the Lord, for he hath triumphed gloriously; the horse and his rider hath he thrown into the sea."

On the right the Lord is showing Moses a tree to throw into the bitter waters of Marah to make them drinkable.

MANNA.   *Exodus xvi* 1-21.

When the people murmured in the wilderness, "the Lord said unto Moses, Behold I will rain bread from heaven for you". Here Moses is standing aside while the people gather diligently and on the right the birds (quails perhaps) are eager for their share.

32

33

MOSES GETTING WATER FROM THE ROCK.　　*Exodus xvii* 1-7.

"He called the name of the place, Massah (Temptation) and Meribah (Chiding) because of the chiding of the children of Israel and because they tempted the Lord, saying, Is the Lord among us or not?"

THE BATTLE WITH AMALEK.　　　　　*Exodus xvii* 8-13.

The first battle with the desert tribes, being fought apparently in the good baronial style of 1478. Not so altogether; for Moses had to have his hands held up by Aaron and Hur to keep the advantage on the side of Israel.

34

35

THE TEN COMMANDMENTS.   *Exodus xix, xx.*
    The Israelites are encamped at the foot of Mount Sinai.
Moses, surrounded by the cloud on the top of the mountain,
is receiving the "tables of stone, written with the finger of
God". (Exodus xxxi 18.)

BEZALEEL AND AHOLIAH.   *Exodus xxxi* 1-11.
    These were the smiths "filled with the spirit of God, in
wisdom . . . and in all manner of workmanship, to devise
cunning works, to work in gold, and in silver, and in brass,
and in cutting of stones and in carving of timber", for the
tabernacle and the ark and all their furniture.

36

37

THE GOLDEN CALF. *Exodus xxxii* 1-6.

While Moses is delayed in the Mount, Aaron yields to the demand for tangible gods, and collects from the people ear-rings which are melted down and made into a golden calf. "And they said, These be thy gods, O Israel, which brought thee up out of the land of Egypt." The sequel fills the rest of the chapter.

"STRANGE FIRE." *Leviticus* x 1-ʒ.

Nadab and Abihu, sons of Aaron, each of them taking his censer and fire therein with incense, and offering "strange fire before the Lord, which he commanded them not"—with the result that "there went out fire from the Lord, and devoured them, and they died before the Lord". Apparently they ought to have lit their censers from the sacred lamp which was kept ever alight in the tabernacle. This is the only *scene* from the Book of Leviticus, a book which is chiefly concerned with ritual.

38

39

NUMBERING THE PEOPLE.   *Numbers i* 1-4.

The Book of Numbers takes its name from this, the first episode in it. It was registration for military service. The queue can be seen stretching far into the distance.

THE SILVER TRUMPETS.   *Numbers x* 1-10.

Moses was directed to get two silver trumpets made, each made from a whole piece of silver. They were to be used for summoning assemblies and for signalling on the march.

40

41

ESHCOL.   *Numbers xiii* 23-27.

The spies sent to seek out the land of Canaan returning to camp with a bunch of grapes that it took two men to carry. In their report on the land they said "Surely it floweth with milk and honey; and this is the fruit of it".

REBELLION OF KORAH, DATHAN   *Numbers xvi* 1-35.
AND ABIRAM.

Moses and Aaron with representatives of the people are on one side, while the Lord sends an earthquake to swallow up the rebels in their tents.

42

43

AARON'S ROD.   *Numbers* xvii.

Twelve rods, one for each tribe, are set up in the tabernacle overnight. In the morning one rod "brought forth buds,
and bloomed blossoms, and yielded almonds". That was
Aaron's, for the tribe of Levi. There could be no doubt of the
sanctity of the Levites after that.

BURIAL OF AARON.   *Numbers* xx 22-29.

Aaron is "gathered to his people" in Mount Hor. His
priestly garments are transferred to Eleazar his son.

44

45

THE BRAZEN SERPENT.   *Numbers xxi* 4-9.

On their journey through the wilderness, the Israelites
come on a place where they are bitten by "fiery serpents".
In answer to his prayer Moses is directed to set up a brazen
image of a "fiery serpent and set it upon a pole; and it shall
come to pass that every one that is bitten, when he looketh
on it, shall live".

BALAAM'S ASS.   *Numbers xxii to xxiv.*

"Balaam who loved the wages of unrighteousness; but was
rebuked for his iniquity; the dumb ass speaking with man's
voice forbad the madness of the prophet." (2 Peter ii 16.)

It is a long story—but perhaps the finest in the Book of
Numbers.

46

47

INDUCTION OF JOSHUA.   *Numbers xxvii* 18-23.
Joshua is to succeed Moses in the leadership. Here Moses
lays his hands upon him and gives him "a charge, as the
Lord commanded". Joshua seems very young to take such
responsibility.

BURIAL OF MOSES.   *Deuteronomy xxxiv* 5, 6.
"So Moses the servant of the Lord died there in the land
of Moab, according to the word of the Lord. And he buried
him in a valley in the land of Moab, over against Bethpeor:
but no man knoweth of his sepulchre unto this day."

48

49

THE FALL OF JERICHO.   *Joshua vi.*
The ark at the head of the army is being carried around
the city seven times. "And it came to pass at the seventh
time, when the priests blew with the trumpets, Joshua said
unto the people, Shout; for the Lord hath given you the
city." Then the walls fell. The picture might be more
impressive; the army is out of sight and the trumpets are
hardly noticeable.

JOSHUA'S TRIUMPH.   *Joshua x 26.*
The awful barbarity of the Book of Joshua is well shown
in this picture.

50

51

GIDEON.   *Judges vi and vii.*

Two scenes: (1) Ch. vi 36-40, Gideon communing with
God and seeking a sign by the formation of dew upon the
fleece; (2) Ch. vii 1-8, Gideon standing by the brook to watch
his men drinking and select those who "lapped" using their
hands.

JEPHTHAH'S DAUGHTER.   *Judges xi 29-40.*

Jephthah had made a rash vow that, if he returned
victorious, the first living creature to come to meet him
should be offered up in sacrifice. And it was his daughter, his
only child. She came to meet him "with timbrels and
dances". He dared not go back on his vow; and indeed she
herself held him to it. All she asked was a respite of two
months to spend in the company of her fellows on the
mountain side. "And it was a custom in Israel that the
daughters of Israel went yearly to lament the daughter of
Jephthah the Gileadite four days in a year."

52

53

SAMSON AND THE LION.   *Judges xiv* 5, 6.
    Samson, on his way to seek a wife from the Philistine city
of Timnath, meets a young lion who "roared against him"
and caused him to exert his great strength.

SAMUEL'S PARENTS.   1 *Samuel i* 1-20.
    Elkanah had two wives who did not get on well together,
for Peninnah had children but Hannah had none. He loved
Hannah, however, and gave her "a worthy portion" of two
doves for her sacrifice at the Tabernacle in Shiloh. When she
returned from Shiloh "the Lord remembered her" and she
bore a son, Samuel, whom she dedicated to the service of
the Lord.

54

55

DEATH OF ELI.   1 *Samuel iv.*

The Israelites, at war with the Philistines, had brought the
Ark of the Covenant into their camp to revive their flagging
spirits; but the Philistines made a determined attack, heavily
defeated the Israelites and, worst of all, carried off the Ark.
Eli, the high priest, now very old and blind, sat by the gate
of Shiloh waiting for news. When told of the defeat and
slaughter of his people, including his two sons, he bore it
well, but when he heard the Ark of God was taken, he fell
off his seat backwards and broke his neck.

The following chapters relate how the Ark brought not
luck to the Philistines, but pestilence, carried presumably by
rats or mice. That appears to be the meaning of the swarm
of small animals making for the city in the distance.

SAMUEL ANOINTING SAUL.   1 *Samuel x 1.*

The story of Samuel's first meeting with Saul is told at
great length in Chapters ix and x. This anointing scene,
outside the city, is the climax. It was still too early for Saul
to be decked with a crown, but kings had to have crowns in
the days when this picture was drawn.

56

57

SAMUEL ANOINTING DAVID.   1 *Samuel* xvi.

Samuel, having found Saul less pliable than he wished, set about finding a successor and proceeded to Bethlehem where he met the elders who accompanied him to the house of Jesse. There he passed in review and rejected seven of Jesse's sons and then made them send out for David, the youngest, "who was ruddy and withal of a beautiful countenance and goodly to look to. And the Lord said, Arise, anoint him; for this is he". The chapter goes on to tell of David's skill with the harp; so the harp is included in the picture.

DAVID AND GOLIATH.   1 *Samuel* xvii.

Such a well-known story scarcely needs comment. In the porch of the mediaeval castle we see Saul offering David his armour. There are spectators on the battlements and the smooth stone can be seen in mid-air.

58

59

DEATH OF SAUL. 1 *Sam. xxxi* 1-6 *and* 2 *Sam. i* 1-17.

The Battle of Gilboa is represented in the background by the contest with swords. On the left in the foreground, Saul in despair is falling on his sword. On the right, as related in 2 Samuel i, the Amalekite who claimed to have slain Saul is offering the crown to David, who laments over Saul and Jonathan. We are told that, far from rewarding the deceitful Amalekite, David had him put to death, because according to his own story he had "slain the Lord's anointed".

BRINGING BACK THE ARK. 2 *Samuel vi* 1-5.

This is the procession along the country road, bringing the Ark from Kirjath-jearim, where it had rested since it fell into the hands of the Philistines and was then hastily pushed back across the frontier to avoid the pestilence it brought. Halfway to Jerusalem, we are told, the "oxen" stumbled. The artist has made them a pair of little ponies with a driver of corresponding size.

60

61

THE SIN OF DAVID.   2 *Samuel* xi 2.

David is fascinated by Uriah's wife, Bathsheba, "washing herself". David, in order to possess her, sank to the lowest depths of meanness and tyranny. Later he bitterly repented. Then Bathsheba became the mother of Solomon and wielded great influence at court.

—

DEATH OF ABSALOM.   2 *Samuel* xviii 1-18.

Absalom having supplanted his father, David, is defeated in battle and while fleeing is caught in a tree by his profuse hair, of which he was inordinately proud. His pursuers catch up with him and, in spite of the king's orders, speedily put him to death.

62

63

MURDER OF AMASA.   2 *Samuel* xx 10.
STAYING OF THE PESTILENCE.   2 *Samuel* xxiv 15-17.

These two scenes are not in any way connected. The murder of Amasa, Absalom's general, by a treacherous stab in the back from Joab, David's general, was an aftermath of the civil war which had just ended.

The pestilence came later, after David had numbered the people. It covered the country from end to end until when "the angel stretched out his hand upon Jerusalem to destroy it, the Lord repented him of this evil". Then David, having laid down his harp and his head-dress, prayed that punishment should fall upon himself and not on the innocent "sheep".

SOLOMON AND BATHSHEBA.   1 *Kings ii* 10-19.

On the left: "So David slept with his fathers and was buried in the city of David". On the right, Solomon upon the throne receives Bathsheba, his mother, and raises her up to sit at his right hand. She is interceding for Adonijah, the favourite for the succession whom Solomon, with the help of Bathsheba, had displaced. Her intercession was in vain; when she came to the point of asking a special favour for Adonijah, Solomon was visibly annoyed and Adonijah was put to death.

64

65

THE JUDGMENT OF SOLOMON.   1 *Kings iii* 16-28
The well-known story showing Solomon's wisdom. There
are two mothers, the child of one having died and the living
child being claimed by both. The executioner is waiting to
carry out Solomon's order to "divide the living child in two,
and give half to the one, and half to the other". The woman
on the right accepts the judgment. The other offers to give
her the child rather than have it slain. "Then the king
answered and said, Give her the living child, and in no wise
slay it; she is the mother thereof." The general public, as
well as the courtiers, are much impressed.

THE QUEEN OF SHEBA.   1 *Kings* x 1-13.
The Queen of Sheba is being given a conducted tour of the
Palace and a crowd has assembled outside, as we might
expect.

66

67

WAR BETWEEN JUDAH AND ISRAEL.   1 *Kings xiv* 30.

After the death of Solomon the kingdom split up "and there was war between Rehoboam and Jeroboam all their days".

This Bible was printed about the time of the Wars of the Roses in England, and the weapons and armour are those of that period.

ELIJAH AND ELISHA.   2 *Kings* ii.

Two scenes: on the left Elijah going up to heaven in the chariot of fire, letting fall his mantle on Elisha; on the right, the dreadful story of the naughty children being eaten up by bears.

68

69

NAAMAN THE SYRIAN.   2 *Kings* v 1-19.
This picture illustrates what is perhaps the finest story in
the Old Testament. It requires no explanation.

ELISHA'S BONES.   2 *Kings* xiii 20, 21.
Elisha had an amazing reputation as a worker of miracles.
Even his dead bones seem to have been effective in restoring
a man to life during an interrupted funeral. The Moabites
responsible for the interruption are riding in on the left.

70

71

AHAZ SACRIFICING. 2 *Kings* xvi 10-13.

Ahaz had been to Damascus to make his peace with the Assyrian King, Tiglath-pileser, who had then just overthrown the kingdom of Syria and carried its people into captivity. In Damascus Ahaz saw an altar of which he sent a plan to the priest in Jerusalem, who had one made for Ahaz against his return home. Ahaz is seen sacrificing at the new altar.

The next chapter, 2 Kings xvii, tells of the overthrow by Assyria of Samaria, the capital of the adjacent kingdom of Israel, and the captivity of its king and people. The background of this picture shows a king and others being led away captive over a bridge.

DESTRUCTION OF SENNACHERIB. 2 *Kings* xviii 13-xix 37.

The left of the picture represents Ch. xix v. 35 when "the angel of the Lord went out and smote the camp of the Assyrian", who had "come down like the wolf on the fold". In the top right hand corner is a king, most likely Hezekiah, with perhaps one of his ministers, looking down on the scene. The story is repeated in almost identical words in the Book of Isaiah and one of its chief features is the contest of oratory between Rabshakeh, the Assyrian general, trying to persuade the Jews to surrender, and the prophet Isaiah, Hezekiah's trusted adviser, encouraging him to hold out. It was the great triumph of Isaiah's career. What happened to Isaiah in the end is not recorded in the Bible, but there is a verse in the Epistle to the Hebrews (xi, 37) implying that certain prophets were "sawn asunder", and there was a legend that this was the fate of Isaiah under Hezekiah's successor. That explains the gruesome picture at the bottom right-hand corner.

72

73

BURIAL OF JOSIAH.   2 *Chronicles* xxxv 24, 25.

King Josiah died of his wounds after the Battle of Megiddo
in which he had unwisely taken part. After this the kingdom
of Judah went to pieces, and he was sorely lamented. Here
he is being buried, with lamentation, in "one of the
sepulchres of his fathers".

EZRA BEFORE DARIUS.   *Ezra vi.*

The picture shows Ezra (Esdre is a Greek form of his
name) kneeling before the great king. There is no record of
such an incident in the Book of Ezra. In earlier chapters of
the book, Darius figures as the just ruler to whom the Jews
appealed when molested by their enemies, and in Ch. vi, to
which this picture is attached, he makes a decree for their
protection. Ezra, however, does not appear until Ch. vii and
then Darius is no longer king, his son Artaxerxes having
succeeded him.

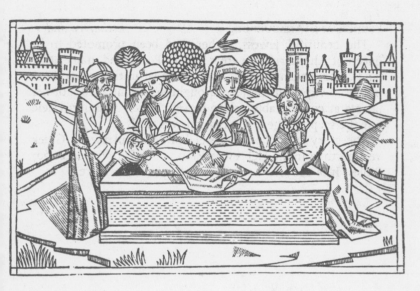

74

75

ESTHER AND AHASUERUS.   *Esther iv and v.*

The beautiful Jewess, Esther, had been promoted to be queen of Ahasuerus, the great king of Persia and many other lands. Her Jewish faith was not disclosed until a court conspiracy to wipe out the Jews brought her to intercede for her people at considerable risk to herself. When Ahasuerus held out the sceptre, she knew that all was well.

The story is told in more elaborate detail in the Greek version than in the Hebrew version which is followed in our Bibles. It is the Greek version that is followed here.

THE AFFLICTION OF JOB.   *Job i 1 to ii 10.*

The Book of Job is a long philosophical poem based upon an imaginary situation in which a good man suffers all kinds of calamities. On the right we see hostile bands of Sabeans or Chaldeans driving off the camels and the flocks and herds, while in the distance "a great wind from the wilderness" has smitten the house in which Job's family were feasting, and crushed them all. On the left Job who has been stricken with disease is sitting naked among ashes, while his wife gives him little comfort by advising him to "curse God and die".

76

77

THE FIERY FURNACE. *Daniel iii.*

The Three Children, Shadrach, Meshach and Abednego, are seen in the furnace unscathed, while the men whose duty it was to thrust them in are overcome by the heat.

THE VISION OF FOUR BEASTS. *Daniel vii 1-8.*

Chapters vii to xii of the Book of Daniel contain a series of prophetic visions relating to the political history of the "Middle East" from about 500 B.C. to 100 B.C. The effect of the various conquests upon the Jewish state is also indicated.

The first vision is that of the four beasts coming up from the sea one after the other. They represent the four empires that dominated Palestine in turn. Babylon, on the right, was like a lion with eagle's wings. Next to it comes the kingdom of the Medes and Persians represented by a bear "devouring much flesh". This was extinguished by the conquests of Alexander of Macedon, whose empire split into four parts, and finally, so far as Palestine was concerned, these were overcome by Rome, the fourth beast, on the left, terrible in its strength and fierceness.

78

79

THE VISION OF THE RAM AND THE HE-GOAT.   *Daniel viii.*
The whole chapter is devoted to the vision and its explanation. Daniel is by the river of Ulai near Shushan, the Palace
in the province of Elam. As described in v. 17, he is falling
on his face before the angel Gabriel to receive the inter-
pretation of the encounter between the ram and the he-goat
seen in the background. The ram, he is told, represents the
kings of Media and Persia and the he-goat the king of Greece.

80

THE APOCRYPHA

The Cologne Bible, and others like it, were simply translations of the Vulgate (or Latin Bible) into modern speech. Jerome about 400 A.D. had translated the Old Testament from the original Hebrew where possible, but had also used the Septuagint, that is the Greek version made for the Jews living in countries where Greek was spoken in the third century B.C. A substantial part of the Septuagint was to be found only in the Greek. These later writings were received without much question by the Western Church, and in the Vulgate they were in no way distinguished from the rest of the Old Testament. They contain, however, some extravagant tales which the Jews have always looked upon not as true stories, but as good fiction having some moral value.

Luther and other translators of the Bible at the time of the Reformation thought it safer to put these writings in a separate section known as the Apocrypha and, where they still survive in bibles used in Protestant churches, that is where they are placed. In most bibles for common use by Protestants they are omitted altogether. In modern English the word "apocryphal" has come to have the meaning of "unlikely to be true".

The Book of Daniel was written partly in Hebrew and partly in Aramaic (the language of Palestine in the time of Jesus) as well as in Greek, but there are two extra Greek chapters which are now included in the Apocrypha. These contain the story of Susanna and an elaboration of the story of Daniel and the Lions' Den under the name of Bel and Dragon.

SUSANNA: "DANIEL COME TO JUDGMENT".   *Daniel xiii.*

This is the story in the Apocrypha regarding Susanna, a virtuous woman falsely accused by two highly respectable elders and hastily condemned. Before sentence could be carried out, the young man Daniel came upon the scene and took charge of the case, convicted the elders of perjury and had them executed instead.

DANIEL IN THE LIONS' DEN.   *Daniel vi and xiv.*

The picture shows on the left Daniel in an upper room of his own house praying to his God, while his jealous rivals are appealing to King Darius to enforce the "law of the Medes and Persians" recently made against this practice. The King having yielded, we see on the right Daniel consigned to the den amid seven hungry lions. Then comes the apocryphal story, of the prophet Habakkuk being brought by an angel from a harvest field in Judaea to drop the reapers' dinner for Daniel and strengthen his faith.

81

82

TOBIT STRICKEN WITH BLINDNESS.   *Tobit ii* 9, 10.

The Book of Tobit is an edifying tale. There is no reason to suppose it was ever intended to be taken as historical fact. This is the first incident. Tobit, an elderly Jew living in Nineveh in the time of Sennacherib, is kept busy relieving the distress of his fellow countrymen in exile in that city. Overcome with sleep he lies down in a recess of the wall of his house and sparrows in the roof drop warm dung into his eyes and blind him. His wife, Anna, and his son Tobias look after him. In these pictures "thobye" is used for both father and son.

TOBIAS AND THE ANGEL.   *Tobit vi.*

Tobit being in need of money sends Tobias to recover a debt owed him by Gabael, a merchant or banker of Rages in Media. For a guide he had the good fortune to meet with and hire the angel Raphael. At the broad River Tigris, Tobias catches a fish, and under Raphael's direction he preserves its heart and liver for use as a medicine or charm. In Media Tobias stayed with his kinsman Raguel and his wife, Edna, and fell in love with their beautiful daughter Sara, whom he proceeded to marry. The nuptials were interfered with by an evil spirit who was scared off as far as Egypt by the smell from the burning entrails of the fish.

83

84

RETURN OF TOBIAS.   *Tobit xi.*

When Tobias had received the money due, he returned home with the angel and with Sara his wife. His first action was to use the fish medicine to anoint the eyes of his father, whose sight was then restored.

Tobias had a dog who ran after him (Ch. xi 4). The artist of these pictures is evidently interested in animals, but has left this one out. This is all the more remarkable in that "Dog Toby" was a regular character in the miracle plays in which scenes from the Bible were enacted in the Middle Ages.

JUDITH.   *Judith xiii.*

Judith, like Tobit, is an "edifying" tale rather than a true story. It is very horrifying too. Holofernes, the general of Nebuchadnezzar's army, was besieging the city in which Judith lived. She was a virtuous widow, but prepared to risk her honour to save her country. She therefore made love to Holofernes and when he was "filled with wine", she took his sword, smote his head off, and dropped it into a bag which she and her maid had ready for the purpose. They got away under pretence of going to prayer and she was hailed in the city as a national heroine.

85

86

THE WAR ELEPHANT.   1 *Maccabees* vi 30.

The two Books of Maccabees are about the Jewish struggle for independence in the second century B.C. At that time elephants were used in battle. The Cologne artist dressed his soldiers in the armour they might have worn in his own day. He had probably never seen an elephant, though he may have read or heard a description of one.

RE-KINDLING THE HOLY FIRE.   2 *Maccabees* i 17-30.

The Second Book of Maccabees opens with a letter addressed to the Jews scattered abroad asking for their support in the struggle for independence about to open. They are reminded of an apocryphal story of Nehemiah re-kindling the holy fire upon the restored temple and altar after the return from the Babylonian exile. The fire had been secretly hidden away for many years and when re-discovered it had turned into "thick water". Nehemiah took this water and poured it on the wood for the sacrifice, whereupon the the sun shone upon it and set the wood alight. This is the moment chosen for the illustration.

87

88

WAR IN THE SKY.   2 *Maccabees* v 1-4.

Antiochus, the King of Syria, was preparing a naval expedition against Egypt, starting from the coast of Palestine. The noise of war preparations was such that the Jews thought they saw troops of horsemen fighting one another in the sky.

The Books of Maccabees are full of horrors and it is perhaps as well that they are but feebly illustrated.

89

THE NEW TESTAMENT

It is remarkable that the bible illustrators, who had taken such pains to depict the stories of the Old Testament, should have done so little for the narrative section of the New. The fact is that in the Middle Ages the Old Testament was regarded as a pre-figuration of the New, and in the Church's teaching the stories from it were valued not so much for their own sake as for their analogy with New Testament incidents celebrated at Christmas, Easter or Whitsuntide. The illustrator of the Cologne Bible would therefore have a considerable stock of commonly accepted analogues on which to draw. On the other hand the mediaeval Church seems to have concentrated so much on the divinity of Christ as to by-pass almost completely his ministry on earth. That seems to be the reason why, instead of illustrations of the life of Christ or his parables, we are given only a heading for each Gospel in which the evangelist is symbolically represented together with some slight indication—not always accurate—of the contents of his work.

A curious convention had grown up around the evangelists. The first chapter of the Book of Ezekiel gives a glowing account of a vision in which the prophet saw four living creatures and two wheels—a wheel within a wheel—controlled from Heaven by the spirit of the Lord. The four living creatures (or beasts) re-appear in the Book of Revelation, and the early Fathers of the Church tried hard to understand what they were supposed to mean. One hit on the idea that they corresponded to the four evangelists, Matthew, Mark, Luke and John. Their faces, we are told, were those of a man, a lion, an ox and an eagle. Now the Gospel of Matthew begins with the visit of an angel, who would have the face of a man. Mark leads off with "a voice crying in the wilderness"—the lion perhaps. Luke starts with a priest offering up a sacrifice—usually taking the form of a calf or an ox. John says, "In the beginning was the

Word"—the winged Word. the eagle. All very artificial and hardly convincing; but the idea took such firm hold in Christian art that the four living creatures were set as symbols, each alongside its own evangelist, for more than fifteen hundred years.

The Epistles do not readily lend themselves to illustration; so it is not surprising that we have nothing more than half-size headings showing Paul entrusting a letter to a messenger, by whom it is duly delivered.

The Book of Revelation in the first edition of the Cologne Bible had only an unsatisfactory heading depicting the supposed martyrdom of John. The second edition had, however, eight full-size illustrations bringing out many of the features of the dream in considerable detail. Prototypes of these have recently been identified in a manuscript in the Bibliothèque Nationale in Paris. The ideas furnished by this manuscript seem also to have been used by Albrecht Dürer for his well-known set of illustrations for the Book of Revelation, which were printed at Strassburg in 1502.

MATTHEW. *Matthew i* 1-17.

Matthew is writing, guided by his angel. The first thing he writes is "the generation of Jesus Christ, the son of David, the son of Abraham". In it he sets out the genealogy in three stages from Abraham to Joseph, the husband of Mary. The persons involved are represented in a procession three deep.

MARK.

Mark is writing with his winged lion at his feet. The scene represented is the Resurrection, Jesus bursting from the tomb, the watchman being stunned as described in Matthew (not in Mark). In the background is Samson carrying the gates of Gaza (Judges xvi 3); this was often taken to be a "pre-figuring" of the resurrection of Jesus Christ.

90

91

LUKE. *Matthew ii 11 and Luke ii 7 and 22.*
Luke is shown writing, with his symbolic calf beside him.
The scenes of the Birth of Jesus and his Presentation in the
Temple are from Luke's Gospel. The visit of the Three Wise
Men bringing gifts occurs only in Matthew.

JOHN. *John i 1-5.*
John, sitting with his eagle, is preparing to write and
seems to be contemplating a vision of the Trinity. The
Father and the Son, seated in Heaven, have between them
"the Word", a bound volume with seven seals. Above them
is a dove representing the Holy Ghost. Below is inset a tiny
view of a pleasing terrestial landscape with a church set in
a valley.

92

93

EPISTLES OF PAUL.

Each of these pictures shows Paul with the "Sword of the Spirit" (Eph. vi 12), which was commonly used as his symbol in mediaeval art. His sword is in his left hand, and with the right he is handing a letter to a messenger. In the background we see the messenger delivering it within a walled city.

In the left hand picture the city is labelled ROM. In the first edition of the Cologne Bible this picture is used for a heading to each of Paul's Epistles. In the second edition it was used only for Romans, to which it properly belongs, and for the other epistles was replaced by the more sophisticated picture on the right.

Unlike the other illustrations of this Bible, these woodcuts had the breadth of one column only.

THE FOUR HORSEMEN.   *Revelation vi 1-8.*

The Book of Revelation is a fantastic dream and it is not easy to follow all the details. The Cologne artist has followed the description closely as regards the four horsemen. The fourth horseman is made to cover the "fourth part of the earth" bringing death to people of all ranks with the sword, the scourge of pestilence and famine, and the terror of a very wild beast.

94

95

THE DAY OF THE WRATH.   *Revelation vi 9 to vii* 14.

This picture is in three sections; first on the left, "under the altar the souls of them that are slain for the testimony which they held". White robes have been given them. Secondly, left of centre, the earthquake when "the kings of the earth, and the great men, and every bondman, and every free man, hid themselves in the dens and the rocks of the mountains". Thirdly, the right half of the picture, "four angels standing on the four corners of the earth holding the four winds". Within their protection is a great multitude, with seals on their foreheads, standing before the throne, clothed with white robes. "These are they which came out of great tribulation, and have washed their robes and made them white in the blood of the Lamb."

THE ADORATION OF THE LAMB.   *Revelation vii* 9-12 *and*
THE FIRST BLASTS OF THE TRUMPET.   *Revelation viii* 6-9.

This picture comes at the end of Chapter ix, but seems to be based on scenes from Chapters vii and viii. God is sitting above the rainbow with the Lamb, surrounded by an adoring multitude among whom the "Four Beasts" can be discerned. In the right half, God is above the altar holding three trumpets, four having been given to four angels. In the distance, in answer to the first trumpet, "hail and fire mingled with blood" fall upon the earth; in the foreground in answer to the second trumpet there is a disturbance on the sea.

96

97

THE TERROR OF THE LOCUSTS.   *Revelation ix* 1-12.

In the centre we see the star falling to earth and the key of the bottomless pit from which smoke rises to blot out the sun. From the pit issue fantastic beasts, whose mission was not to hurt the vegetation "but only those men which have not the seal of God in their foreheads". It will be noticed that the victims embrace a variety of ordinary men together with dignitaries of church and state, not excluding the Pope with his tiara. The saints, who have the seal of God, look on unharmed.

THE SIXTH WOE AND THE PILLARED ANGEL.   *Rev. ix* 13-*x* 11.

"The sixth angel which had the trumpet" is in the top left hand corner. The effect of the blast is to let loose an army of horsemen with breastplates of fire riding on horses with heads of lions, out of whose mouths issue fire and smoke and brimstone. Among those who perish are the Pope and the Emperor.

On the right comes the pillared angel, carefully modelled on the description in Chapter x. He is clothed with a cloud. He has one foot on sea and one on land. With his right hand held up to heaven he is swearing "that there should be time no longer". With his left he hands a "little book" to John, who is kneeling to receive it.

98

99

THE TWO WITNESSES.   *Revelation* xi 1-14 *and*
THE WOMAN IN TRAVAIL.   *Revelation* xii 1-5.
On the left we see John with a rod about to measure the
temple and altar. Beside him are "Gentiles" in the outer
court. Next above them come the "two witnesses clothed in
sackcloth" and, almost in line, the "two candlesticks standing before the God of the earth". The witnesses are facing the
beast, who seems responsible for the "war" in which they are
killed. Above we see them again in a cloud in heaven, and
the "tenth part of the city" falling in an earthquake.
On the right we have the "woman clothed with the sun
and the moon under her feet", faced by the "great red
dragon, having seven heads and ten horns, and seven crowns
upon his heads", his tail sweeping the stars from heaven.
In the top right hand corner is the man child, whom she
brought forth, "caught up to God and to his throne".

WAR IN HEAVEN.   *Revelation* xii 7-10 *and*
THE BEAST.   *Revelation* xiii.
On the left the Archangel Michael is fighting against the
dragon called also the Devil or Satan, and casting him out
into the earth. There are two different versions of "the
Beast". That with seven heads and ten horns occupies the
centre of the picture and the other one "with two horns like
unto a lamb" is at the right hand side, with fire dropping
from heaven. Their worshippers are also shown. In the
bottom right hand corner is the war against the saints, who
are overcome (Ch. xiii 7).

100

101

THE SCARLET WOMAN AND HER DOWNFALL.

Revelation xiv, xvii, xviii, xx.

Chapter xvii 9 gives a clear indication that the Scarlet Woman sitting on the dragon with seven heads is symbolic of Imperial Rome. She goes by the name of Babylon, first of all in Chapter xiv 8. On the left of the picture we see her as described in Chapter xvii sitting "upon many waters", having a golden cup in her hand, worshipped by the minor kings of the earth. Her walls are toppling.

The centre is taken from Chapter xvii 21-24, the angel dropping the great millstone into the sea. Next comes the angel with the key of the bottomless pit to which "that old serpent, which is the Devil and Satan" is about to be consigned (Ch. xx 1, 2).

On the right we have the closing scenes of Chapter xiv, the harvest of the world and the vintage of the grapes of wrath.

102

INDEX OF ILLUSTRATIONS

GENERAL INDEX